pasta

pasta

TIME
LIFE
BOOKS

Alexandria, Virginia

TIME®
LIFE
BOOKS

Time-Life Books is a division of Time Life Inc.
Time-Life is a trademark of Time Warner Inc. and affiliated companies.

TIME LIFE INC.
CHAIRMAN AND CHIEF EXECUTIVE OFFICER: Jim Nelson
PRESIDENT AND CHIEF OPERATING OFFICER: Steven Janas

TIME-LIFE BOOKS
PRESIDENT: Larry Jellen
VICE PRESIDENT AND PUBLISHER: Neil S. Levin
VICE PRESIDENT, CONTENT DEVELOPMENT: Jennifer L. Pearce
SENIOR SALES DIRECTOR: Richard J. Vreeland
DIRECTOR, MARKETING AND PUBLICITY: Inger Forland
DIRECTOR OF TRADE SALES: Dana Hobson
DIRECTOR OF CUSTOM PUBLISHING: John Lalor
DIRECTOR OF RIGHTS AND LICENSING: Olga Vezeris
DIRECTOR OF NEW PRODUCT DEVELOPMENT: Carolyn M. Clark
EXECUTIVE EDITOR: Linda Bellamy
DIRECTOR OF DESIGN: Kate L. McConnell
TECHNICAL SPECIALIST: Monika Lynde

PASTA
PROJECT EDITOR: Paula York-Soderlund
DESIGN ASSISTANT: Jody Billert

First published in the U.K. in 1999 by Hamlyn
Octopus Publishing Group Limited, 2–4 Heron Quays, London E14 4JP

Printed in China.
10 9 8 7 6 5 4 3 2 1

School and library distribution by Time-Life Education, P.O. Box 85026, Richmond, Virginia 23285-5026.

Library of Congress Cataloging-in-Publication Data
Pasta : over 60 simple recipes for great home cooking!
      p. cm.
   Includes index
   ISBN 0-7370-2065-2 (hardcover)
   1. Cookery (Pasta) I. Time-Life Books.

TX809.M17 .P3615 2001
641.8'22--dc21   00-051186

Notes
1 Milk should be whole milk unless otherwise stated.
2 Fresh herbs should be used unless otherwise stated. If unavailable, use dried herbs as an alternative but only half the amount stated.
3 Pepper should be freshly ground black pepper unless otherwise stated; season to taste.
4 Do not refreeze a dish that has been frozen previously.

contents

introduction

Pasta has been a staple food for thousands of years. Records show that the Chinese were eating pasta as far back as the Shang dynasty some 3,500 years ago. However, it is the Italians who are the most serious pasta eaters. It is not hard to see why pasta is so popular since it's such a versatile convenience food. Cheap, quick, and easy to cook – and perfectly designed to mix with anything from a drizzle of olive oil and a sprinkling of herbs, to colorful ingredients like olives and tomatoes, or thick sauces made with sausage or fish. Pasta can be served as an appetizer or main course, and used in many different types of dishes, from soups to salads.

Pasta is made from wheat flour and water. The best Italian varieties use durum wheat, a hard wheat which makes a good firm pasta dough. Some doughs are made with eggs and these pastas are called *pasta all'uovo*. When spinach is added to the dough, it is called *pasta verde*, and when tomato is included the pasta is called *pasta rossa*. Wholewheat pasta and buckwheat pasta are also available; both these pastas have a brown color and a more chewy texture, and they are richer in vitamins, minerals, and fiber.

Types of pasta

Pasta is readily available fresh or dried, in an enormous variety of shapes and sizes. Dried pasta, called *pasta secca* in Italian, is particularly useful as it can be stored for months in the kitchen cabinet. It ranges in size from tiny shapes, called pastini, to the large cannelloni tubes, which are ideal for stuffing. The recipes in this book use dried pasta unless fresh is specified. Fresh pastas include ribbon pastas such as tagliatelle, linguine, and spaghetti, and also sheets of pasta for lasagne and cannelloni. Fresh stuffed pastas such as ravioli and tortellini are also now sold in most supermarkets.

The following are just some of the many varieties of pasta available:

Bucatini: thick, tubular spaghetti. Good with thick and smooth sauces.

Cannelloni: large, hollow tubes for stuffing with meat, fish, or vegetables. Can be baked in a sauce.

Capelli d'angelo: also called angel hair pasta; long, very thin vermicelli. Good with smooth sauces and in soups.

Conchiglie: shells in many different sizes. Use with chunky and creamy sauces, and in soups and salads.

Farfalle: also called bows; available fresh or dried. May be flavored with spinach or tomato. Use with sauces and in salads.

Fedelini: also called spaghettini; long, thin spaghetti. Use with smooth and creamy sauces.

'No man is lonely while eating spaghetti;
it requires so much attention.'

Christopher Morley

Fettuccine: long, flat ribbon noodles, sometimes coiled into nests. Use with smooth and creamy sauces.

Fiorelli: short tubes, one end having a lacy edge. Good with chunky sauces.

Fusilli: spirals, coils, or springs, long or short; available fresh or dried; may be flavored with spinach. Use with sauces and in salads.

Gnocchi: small potato dumplings eaten in the same way as pasta.

Lasagne: flat rectangular or square sheets; often ridged or with crinkled edges. Available fresh or dried, they may be flavored with spinach. Use in layers with meat, fish, or vegetables and cheese sauce, in baked dishes, or rolled around filling to make cannelloni.

Linguine: thin, flat, ribbon noodles. Use like spaghetti.

Lumache: snails. Use like conchiglie.

Macaroni: thick, slightly curved, hollow pasta of varying lengths, such as short-cut and elbow macaroni. Quick-cook macaroni is also available. Use with thick and creamy sauces; good in baked dishes.

Noodles: there are many types of oriental noodles made from wheat flour but they tend to be paler in color than Italian varieties. Thin white translucent noodles, made from rice flour or mung bean flour, can be used in soups and sauces, or stir-fried.

Pappardelle: broad egg noodles made in a similar way to tagliatelle, but cut into wider strips. Use like tagliatelle.

Pastini: tiny shapes (for example, anelini, conchigliette, farfallette, orecchiette, and roteline). Use in soups, casseroles, and children's dishes.

Penne: short, tubular pieces of pasta with angled ends. Penne rigate are ridged. Use like short-cut macaroni.

Ravioli: fresh pasta filled with spinach and ricotta cheese. Serve with melted butter or a sauce.

Rigatoni: short-cut, ridged tubes. Use like short-cut macaroni.

Rotelle: also called ruote; shaped like cartwheels or wagon wheels. Good for children's dishes, and in soups, stews, and salads.

Spaghetti: long, thin strings, available fresh or dried. Spaghettini is thinner. Use with any kind of sauce.

Tagliarini: flat ribbon noodles, thinner than tagliatelle, available fresh or dried. May be flavored with tomato, spinach, or egg.

Tagliatelle: flat ribbon noodles, sometimes coiled into nests, available fresh or dried. May be flavored with herbs, spinach, or egg. Good with smooth sauces.

Tortellini: Small, stuffed shapes of fresh pasta with fillings such as tomato and basil. Tortelloni are the same shape only larger. Serve with melted butter or sauce.

Tripolini: small, rounded bows. Good in soups.

Vermicelli: thin pasta strands. Use like spaghetti.

Servings

As a rough guide, allow 3–4 oz. fresh or dried pasta per person for a main course; 2 oz. for an appetizer. The amount depends on whether the pasta is to be served simply, or with a substantial sauce.

Cooking pasta

Pasta is very easy to cook as long as you follow a few simple rules. The most important one is that pasta must be cooked in a large pot in plenty of boiling, salted water, so that it has room to cook without sticking together. Try to use a pot which will hold at least a gallon of water. You can add a little olive oil to the water, if you like – opinions differ as to whether this helps to prevent the pasta strands or shapes from sticking together. When cooking spaghetti, add it all to the pot at the same time, gently pushing the pasta into the boiling water as it softens.

Give the pasta a good stir and keep it at a steady boil while it cooks. Fresh pasta will take 2–3 minutes (5–10 minutes for filled types); dried pasta takes 8–12 minutes though you should always check the package instructions and test the pasta for readiness a little before the suggested time. Pasta is ready when it is *al dente*, an Italian term meaning tender but still firm when bitten. Test by biting a piece or squeeze a piece of it between your fingers; if it breaks cleanly, it is cooked. Do not cook pasta until very soft or it will be mushy by the time you serve it.

Dry pasta swells to almost double its original bulk during cooking so drain it in a colander. Serve cooked pasta at once.

mushroom & boursin tagliatelle ●

oriental pasta salad ●

macaroni with sausage & tomato ●

penne with spicy olive sauce ●

country-style macaroni ●

quick pasta soup ●

smoked chicken & penne rigate ●

penne with turkey & pesto ●

spaghetti with genovese sauce ●

fresh pasta with crab & zucchini ●

asparagus & mushroom tagliatelle ●

spaghetti with tuna sauce ●

tagliatelle with broccoli, shrimp, & scallops ●

quick & easy

mushroom & boursin tagliatelle

1 Bring a large pot of salted water to a boil. Add the pasta and cook for 8–12 minutes or according to the package instructions, until just tender.

2 Meanwhile, make the sauce. Heat the oil in a pan and fry the onion and garlic until softened. Add half the chives, along with the mushrooms and wine. Bring to a boil and cook for 2 minutes, then remove from heat, stir in the boursin and cream, and season to taste. Stir until heated through.

3 Drain the pasta, add it to the sauce, and toss gently to combine everything. Serve garnished with the remaining chives.

12 oz. spinach tagliatelle or fettuccine

1 tablespoon olive oil

1 onion, chopped

2 garlic cloves, crushed

2 tablespoons chopped chives

½ lb. white mushrooms, sliced (about 2⅓ cups)

½ cup dry white wine

2 oz. boursin cheese with pepper (about ¼ cup)

½ cup heavy cream

salt and pepper

Serves 4
Preparation time: 10 minutes
Cooking time: 8–12 minutes

1. Bring a large pot of salted water to a boil. Add the pasta and cook for 8–12 minutes or according to the package instructions, until just tender. Drain, and run under cold water until the pasta is cold.

2. Blanch the snow peas and asparagus in a pot of boiling water for 2 minutes, then drain in a colander. Refresh under cold water, then add to the bowl of pasta along with the carrot, scallions, and the red peppers.

3. In a small, heavy saucepan, heat the sesame and sunflower oils. Add the ginger and sesame seeds and cook for 30–60 seconds until they start to pop. Remove the pan from the heat, stir in the soy sauce, and season to taste with salt and pepper. Pour the dressing over the pasta and toss thoroughly. Serve immediately.

10 oz. caserecce or pasta twists

5 oz. snow peas, trimmed (about 1 large handful)

¼ lb. asparagus tips, cut in half widthwise (about 1 full cup)

1 large carrot, cut into matchsticks

4 scallions, cut into matchsticks

2 red bell peppers, cored, seeded, and cut into strips

2 tablespoons sesame oil

2 tablespoons sunflower oil

1 inch piece of fresh ginger, peeled and finely shredded

2 teaspoons sesame seeds

¼ cup soy sauce

salt and pepper

Serves 4
Preparation time: 10 minutes
Cooking time: 8–12 minutes

oriental pasta salad

14

macaroni with sausage & tomato

1 Cut each sausage into 4 or 5 pieces. Heat the oil in a large pan, add the garlic and onions, and cook until softened and lightly colored.

2 Add the sausage and fry until evenly browned. Add the red peppers, tomatoes, oregano, tomato paste, Marsala or sherry, and salt and pepper to taste. Cook on low heat, uncovered, for 12–15 minutes.

3 Meanwhile, bring a large pot of salted water to a boil. Add the pasta and cook for 8–12 minutes or according to the package instructions, until just tender. Drain well and stir in the butter.

4 Mix the pasta and sauce together and transfer to a warmed serving dish or individual dishes. Serve at once.

½ lb. Italian sausages, skinned

2 tablespoons olive oil

2 garlic cloves, crushed

2 small onions, roughly chopped

2 small red bell peppers, cored, seeded, and cubed

1½ lbs tomatoes, skinned and chopped

2 teaspoons dried oregano

2 tablespoons tomato paste

6 tablespoons Marsala or sherry

8 oz. macaroni

2 tablespoons butter

salt and pepper

Serves 4
Preparation time: 20 minutes
Cooking time: 20 minutes

■ Italian pork sausages have a coarser texture and stronger flavor than regular American sausages. They can be fried or boiled.

penne with spicy olive sauce

1 Bring a large pot of salted water to a boil. Add the pasta and cook for 8–12 minutes or according to the package instructions, until just tender.

2 Drain the pasta and return it to the pot. Add the oil, ginger, nutmeg, garlic, capers, olives, and chopped parsley.

3 Season with salt and pepper and stir over a low heat for 1–2 minutes. Serve at once, garnished with basil sprigs.

1 lb. penne

½ cup olive oil

½ teaspoon ground ginger

pinch of freshly grated nutmeg

1 garlic clove, crushed

3 tablespoons capers

½ cup pitted black olives, sliced

2 tablespoons chopped parsley

salt and pepper

basil sprigs, for garnishing

Serves 4
Preparation time: 10 minutes
Cooking time: 10–15 minutes

1 Soak the anchovy fillets in a little milk for a few minutes to remove the excess salt. Heat the oil in a small pan. Add the whole garlic clove and the drained anchovies. Cook over medium heat for a few minutes, then remove the garlic and add the bacon.

2 Meanwhile, drain the tomatoes and cut into strips. When the bacon is crisp, add the tomatoes to the pan. Season with salt and pepper and let cook over low heat for about 10 minutes. Add the olives and oregano, and continue cooking until a thick sauce has formed.

3 Bring a large pot of salted water to a boil. Add the pasta and cook for 8–12 minutes or according to the package instructions, until just tender. Drain the pasta and transfer to a warmed serving dish, then pour the sauce over it and sprinkle with the grated Romano cheese. Mix well before serving.

2 anchovy fillets

a little milk

¼ cup oil

1 garlic clove

2 oz. bacon, diced (about 4–5 strips)

15 oz. can plum tomatoes

⅓ cup pitted black olives, chopped

¼ teaspoon chopped oregano

12 oz. macaroni

2 tablespoons grated Romano cheese

salt and pepper

Serves 4	
Preparation time: 10–15 minutes	
Cooking time: 25–30 minutes	

country-style macaroni

quick pasta soup

1 Heat the oil in a large pot, add the onion, parsley, vegetables, and tomato paste, and cook for 2 minutes, stirring.

2 Add the hot vegetable stock and bring to a boil. Add the pasta, lower the heat and simmer, covered, for about 8–12 minutes or until the pasta is cooked.

3 Add plenty of salt and pepper to taste. Serve at once with some crusty bread.

1 tablespoon olive oil

1 onion, chopped

2 tablespoons chopped parsley

1½ cups diced mixed vegetables

2 tablespoons tomato paste

5 cups hot vegetable stock

2 oz. conchiglie or other small shells (about ⅔ cup)

salt and pepper

crusty bread, for serving

Serves 4
Preparation time: 2–3 minutes
Cooking time: 10–14 minutes

smoked chicken & penne rigate

1 Bring a large pot of salted water to a boil. Add the pasta and cook for 8–12 minutes or according to the package instructions, until just tender.

2 Meanwhile, heat the oil in a frying pan and add the shallots. Fry for 1 minute, stirring constantly, until softened. Add the mushrooms and fry for 2 minutes more. Lower the heat and add the cheese, breaking it up with the back of a wooden spoon. Stir in the cream, chicken, and parsley. Stir over a low heat for 5 minutes, until thoroughly heated through. Add plenty of salt and pepper to taste.

3 Drain the pasta and drizzle with a little oil. Season with pepper and add to the sauce. Stir well and then serve at once.

12 oz. penne rigate

1 tablespoon olive oil, plus extra for drizzling

2 shallots, finely chopped (or 1 small mild onion)

¼ lb. wild mushrooms, sliced (about 1 cup)

5 oz. Boursin cheese with herbs (about ½ cup)

⅔ cup heavy cream

½ lb. smoked chicken breast, skinned and sliced

2 tablespoons chopped parsley

salt and pepper

Serves 4
Preparation time: 10 minutes
Cooking time: 8–12 minutes

▦ Wild mushrooms are better for this dish than cultivated mushrooms, as they have a stronger flavor, but if they are unavailable, use ordinary white mushrooms.

penne with turkey & pesto

1 Bring a large pot of salted water to a boil. Add the pasta and cook for 8–12 minutes or according to the package instructions, until just tender.

2 Heat a wok or large, deep frying pan and add the oil. Heat until it is hot, but not smoking. Add the turkey and stir-fry for 1–2 minutes. Add the pesto and stir-fry for a further 1–2 minutes, until the turkey is thoroughly heated through.

3 Drain the pasta, add it to the turkey mixture, and toss over high heat until well mixed. Add the cream or crème fraîche and season to taste with salt and pepper. Toss well to mix, then divide among 4 warmed serving plates. Garnish with Parmesan shavings and basil, and serve at once.

10 oz. penne

1 tablespoon olive oil

12 oz. cooked turkey, cut into thin strips

3 tablespoons ready-made pesto

4–6 tablespoons heavy cream or crème fraîche

salt and pepper

For Garnishing:

Parmesan cheese shavings

basil leaves

Serves 4
Preparation time: 5 minutes
Cooking time: 10–14 minutes

spaghetti with genovese sauce

1 Put the garlic cloves, walnuts, basil leaves, Parmesan, and oil into a blender or food processor, and blend until smooth. Season to taste with salt. Otherwise, use a mortar and pestle to pound the garlic with a little salt, then add the walnuts, and then the basil, pounding between each addition to form a smooth paste. Add the cheese and oil and stir well.

2 Bring a large pot of salted water to a boil. Add the pasta and cook for 8–12 minutes or according to the package instructions, until just tender.

3 Drain the pasta, return it to the rinsed-out pot, and stir in half the sauce. Pile the pasta onto a warmed serving dish and serve garnished with basil leaves. Serve the rest of the sauce separately.

3 garlic cloves

½ cup walnuts

1 oz. basil leaves, finely chopped (about ½ cup), plus extra to garnish

1 cup grated Parmesan cheese

⅔ cup olive oil

12 oz. spaghetti or ribbon noodles

salt

Serves 4
Preparation time: 15 minutes
Cooking time: 8–12 minutes

■ This delicious sauce will keep for up to 2 weeks in a screw-top jar in the refrigerator.

fresh pasta with crab & zucchini

1 Cut the zucchini into thin strips. Melt the butter in a large pan, add the garlic and zucchini, and cook for 3 minutes.

2 Meanwhile, bring a large pot of salted water to a boil. Add the pasta and cook for 2–3 minutes or according to the package instructions, until just tender. Drain the pasta and add it to the pan with the zucchini.

3 Add the crab to the pan along with the lemon juice, and season generously with salt and pepper. Stir the ingredients gently to combine them, then cook over a medium heat for 1–2 minutes to heat the crab meat. Serve at once, garnished with lemon wedges and parsley sprigs.

½ lb. small zucchini, trimmed

½ stick (¼ cup) butter

1 garlic clove, crushed

12 oz. fresh pasta, such as linguine

6 oz. white crab meat (about ⅔ cup)

2 teaspoons lemon juice

salt and pepper

For Garnishing:

lemon wedges

parsley sprigs

Serves 4
Preparation time: 10 minutes
Cooking time: 5 minutes

asparagus & mushroom tagliatelle

1 Melt the butter in a large frying pan and add the asparagus, mushrooms, and ginger. Mix gently and let the vegetables cook slowly, without browning, for 5–8 minutes.

2 Add the tarragon and cream or crème fraîche to the pan. Season to taste with salt and pepper. Stir gently, then simmer for 5 minutes.

3 Meanwhile, bring a large pot of salted water to a boil. Add the pasta and cook for 8–12 minutes or according to the package instructions, until just tender.

4 Drain the pasta and return it to the rinsed-out pot. Pour the asparagus and mushroom sauce over the tagliatelle and stir carefully. Transfer to a warmed serving dish and garnish with a few strips of lemon zest and parsley sprigs, if you like. Serve immediately.

2 tablespoons butter

½ lb. fresh asparagus spears, cut into 1 inch lengths, blanched (about 2 cups)

¼ lb. wild mushrooms or white mushrooms, sliced (about 1 cup)

1 inch piece of fresh ginger, peeled and grated

1 tablespoon chopped tarragon

1 cup heavy cream or crème fraîche

12 oz. fresh tagliatelle or fettuccine

salt and pepper

For Garnishing:

strips of lemon zest

parsley sprigs (optional)

Serves 4

Preparation time: 10 minutes

Cooking time: 15–20 minutes

1 Bring a large pot of salted water to a boil. Add the pasta and cook for 8–12 minutes or according to the package instructions, until just tender.

2 Meanwhile, heat the oil and the butter in a pan, add the garlic, and cook over medium heat for 2 minutes. Add the stock and sherry, and boil rapidly for 5 minutes to reduce the liquid. Stir in the tuna, cream, and two-thirds of the parsley. Season with salt and pepper, and stir well to mix.

3 Drain the spaghetti and toss with the sauce. Serve garnished with the remaining parsley.

12 oz. spaghetti

2 tablespoons olive oil

2 tablespoons butter

1 garlic clove, finely chopped

1 cup fish or chicken stock

3 tablespoons dry sherry

6 oz. can tuna, drained and flaked

2 tablespoons light cream

3 tablespoons chopped parsley

salt and pepper

Serves 4
Preparation time: 5 minutes
Cooking time: 15 minutes

spaghetti with tuna sauce

1 lb. tagliatelle or fettuccine verde

14 oz. broccoli flowerets (4–5 cups)

2 tablespoons olive oil

1 tablespoon chopped fresh ginger

2 garlic cloves, thinly sliced

¼ lb. white mushrooms, sliced (about 1 cup)

½ lb. scallops

6 oz. cooked peeled shrimp (about 1⅓ cups)

⅓ cup dry sherry

⅔ cup light cream

1 teaspoon chopped marjoram

1 teaspoon chopped thyme

salt and pepper

Serves 4–6

Preparation time: 5–10 minutes

Cooking time: 8–12 minutes

---

1 Bring a large pot of salted water to a boil. Add the pasta and cook for 8–12 minutes or according to the package instructions, until just tender.

2 Meanwhile, break the broccoli into small flowerets and boil in salted water for 1 minute, then drain and reserve.

3 Heat the oil in a large frying pan, add the ginger and garlic, and brown lightly. Stir in the mushrooms, scallops, and shrimp. Add the sherry and boil rapidly until it is reduced to about 2 tablespoons. Add the cream, herbs, and salt and pepper to taste. Add the broccoli to the sauce and heat thoroughly. Transfer the drained pasta to warmed serving plates, pour the sauce over it and serve immediately.

tagliatelle with broccoli, shrimp, & scallops

baked lasagne ●

spaghetti alla bolognese ●

spaghetti alle vongole ●

spaghetti alla carbonara ●

fettuccine alfredo ●

pasta primavera ●

wholewheat spaghetti marinara ●

tagliatelle with four cheeses ●

penne with spicy sausage sauce ●

smoked haddock & pepper pasta ●

macaroni & cheese ●

pasta classics

baked lasagne

1 To make the white sauce, melt the butter in small saucepan and stir in the flour. Cook over gentle heat for 1–2 minutes, then remove from the heat. Gradually beat in the milk, then return to a low heat. Cook, stirring all the time, until you have a thickened, smooth sauce. Season with salt, pepper, and nutmeg.

2 Butter an ovenproof dish and pour in a little meat sauce. Add a layer of lasagne sheets, then a layer of white sauce and Bel Paese or fontina. Continue to layer the ingredients to fill the dish, finishing with a layer of white sauce.

3 Sprinkle the Parmesan over the top and bake in a preheated oven at 350°F for 40–45 minutes. Serve hot, garnished with sprigs of oregano.

1 quantity Meat Sauce (see opposite), cooked for 20 minutes only

8 oz. dried or fresh lasagne sheets, cooked according to package directions

12 oz. Bel Paese or fontina cheese, thinly sliced or grated

2–3 tablespoons grated Parmesan cheese

oregano sprigs, for garnishing

White Sauce:

3 tablespoons butter

6 tablespoons flour

2½ cups milk

grated nutmeg

salt and pepper

Serves 4
Preparation time: 20 minutes
Cooking time: 1 hour 20 minutes

1 Heat the oil in a large saucepan or deep frying pan, add the onion, garlic, bacon, carrot, and celery, and cook until soft and golden. Add the beef and cook, stirring occasionally, until browned.

2 Add the red wine and bring to a boil. Reduce the heat slightly and cook over a medium heat until most of the wine has evaporated. Season with salt and pepper.

3 Add the milk and a little grated nutmeg, and stir well. Continue cooking until the milk has been absorbed by the meat mixture. Add the tomatoes, sugar, and oregano. Reduce the heat to a bare simmer and cook, uncovered, for about 2–2½ hours until the sauce is well reduced and richly colored.

4 Bring a large pot of salted water to a boil. Add the pasta and cook for 8–12 minutes or according to the package instructions, until just tender. Drain well and season with pepper. Pour the meat sauce over it and serve at once, with the Parmesan passed around separately, if using.

¼ cup olive oil

1 onion, finely chopped

1 garlic clove, crushed

4 strips of bacon chopped

1 carrot, diced

1 celery stalk, diced

1 lb. lean ground beef

⅔ cup red wine

½ cup milk

freshly grated nutmeg

14 oz. can chopped tomatoes

1 tablespoon sugar

1 teaspoon chopped oregano

1 lb. spaghetti

salt and pepper

1 cup grated Parmesan cheese, for garnishing (optional)

Serves 4
Preparation time: 15 minutes
Cooking time: 2½–3 hours

spaghetti alla bolognese

1 Put the clams in a large pot with the water. Cook until the shells open, then remove the clams from the shells. Strain the cooking liquid and set aside for later.

2 Heat the oil in a heavy pan, add the garlic, and cook gently for 5 minutes. Remove the garlic, then add the tomatoes and the reserved cooking liquid to the pan. Stir, and simmer for 20 minutes.

3 Meanwhile, bring a large pot of salted water to a boil. Add the pasta and cook for 8–12 minutes or according to the package instructions, until just tender. Drain thoroughly.

4 Add the clams and parsley to the tomato sauce and heat thoroughly for 1 minute. Pile the spaghetti in a warmed serving dish, add the sauce and a pinch of pepper, and fork gently to mix. Serve at once.

2 lbs. fresh clams, scrubbed under cold running water

½ cup water

½ cup olive oil

1 garlic clove, sliced

14 oz. tomatoes, skinned and crushed (about 3½ cups)

14 oz. spaghetti

1 tablespoon chopped parsley

salt and pepper

Serves 4
Preparation time: 20 minutes
Cooking time: 40 minutes

spaghetti alle vongole

■ To peel tomatoes, put them in a bowl and cover with boiling water for 15 seconds, then lift out with a slotted spoon and plunge into cold water. Drain them and peel off the skins.

spaghetti alla carbonara

1 Bring a large pot of salted water to a boil. Add the pasta and cook for 8–12 minutes or according to the package instructions, until just tender.

2 Meanwhile, heat the oil in a large heavy pot. Add the bacon and cook over medium heat until cooked and golden brown.

3 Drain the pasta and add it to the bacon. Gently stir in the beaten eggs and cream. Season to taste with salt and pepper. Stir over very low heat until the eggs start to set.

4 Toss the spaghetti lightly with most of the Parmesan and serve at once while still hot, sprinkled with the remaining Parmesan and the parsley, if using.

1 lb. spaghetti

2 tablespoons olive oil

8 strips of bacon, chopped

3 eggs, beaten

3 tablespoons light cream

1 cup grated Parmesan cheese

salt and pepper

2 tablespoons chopped parsley, for garnishing (optional)

Serves 4
Preparation time: 5 minutes
Cooking time: 15–20 minutes

fettuccine alfredo

1 Bring a large pot of salted water to a boil. Add the pasta and cook for 8–12 minutes or according to the package instructions, until just tender.

2 Meanwhile, melt the butter in a very large frying pan. Add the onion and garlic and fry over high heat for 1 minute, stirring constantly.

3 Warm the cream in a saucepan. Pour it over the onion mixture and add the nutmeg. Bring the mixture to a boil, add salt and pepper to taste, then remove from the heat.

4 Drain the pasta and add it to the sauce. Push the pasta to one side of the pan, return it to a low heat, and, in the available space, beat the egg, and stir it into the pasta. While the mixture is cooking, add the Parmesan. Stir well and as soon as the cheese has melted, tip the fettuccine onto warmed plates. Serve at once, garnished with parsley.

10 oz. fettuccine

2 tablespoons butter

1 onion, finely chopped

3 garlic cloves, finely chopped

2 cups light cream

½ teaspoon grated nutmeg

1 egg, beaten

1 cup grated Parmesan cheese

salt and pepper

1 tablespoon chopped parsley, for garnishing

Serves 4
Preparation time: 10 minutes
Cooking time: 15 minutes

pasta primavera

1 Bring two pots of water to a boil and cook the green vegetables in one and the carrot in the other, until tender but still crisp. Transfer the vegetables to ice water to stop them cooking. Drain well and pat dry with paper towels.

2 Bring a large pot of salted water to a boil. Add the pasta and cook for 8–12 minutes or according to the package instructions, until just tender.

3 Meanwhile, melt the butter with the oil in a large frying pan over medium heat. Add the red pepper and fry for 1 minute. Add the pine nuts and fry for a further minute. Add the cooked vegetables and toss until they are well coated with oil, and warmed right through.

4 Drain the pasta and transfer it to a warm serving bowl. Add the hot vegetables with the shredded lettuce and chives, and toss well. Add salt to taste, and toss again. Garnish with the parsley, sprinkle with the Parmesan, and serve at once.

½ lb. snow peas, trimmed (about 2 large handfuls)

½ lb. fresh asparagus (optional)

6 oz. thin green beans, cut into pieces 1¼ inches long (1⅓ cups)

1 carrot, cut into thin strips

12 oz. spaghetti

2 tablespoons butter

¼ cup olive oil

1 red bell pepper, cored, seeded, and diced

2 tablespoons pine nuts, toasted

½ small Boston lettuce, shredded

2 tablespoons chopped chives

salt

For Garnishing:

¼ cup finely chopped parsley

freshly grated Parmesan cheese

Serves 4–6
Preparation time: 10 minutes
Cooking time: 30–40 minutes

▨ Other green vegetables may be substituted. Try zucchini, fresh peas, or broccoli instead, if you like.

wholewheat spaghetti marinara

1 Bring a large pot of salted water to a boil. Add the pasta and cook for 8–12 minutes or according to the package instructions, until just tender.

2 Meanwhile, heat the oil in a large frying pan, add the onion, and fry gently for 5 minutes until softened. Add the wine and garlic, and simmer until the liquid is reduced by one-third. Add the cream or crème fraîche, chives, shrimp, and mussels. Heat through gently and season to taste with salt and pepper.

3 Drain the pasta and divide it among 4 warmed serving plates. Spoon the sauce over the top, and sprinkle with chives. Serve the pasta at once, with Parmesan passed round separately.

12 oz. wholewheat spaghetti

2 tablespoons olive oil

1 onion, chopped

1¼ cups dry white wine

1 garlic clove, crushed

⅔ cup heavy cream or crème fraîche

2 tablespoons chopped fresh chives, plus extra to garnish

6 oz. cooked peeled shrimp (about 1⅓ cups)

8 oz. canned or frozen mussels

salt and pepper

Parmesan cheese, for serving

Serves 4
Preparation time: 10 minutes
Cooking time: 15 minutes

■ Fresh mussels may be used instead. Steam in a little wine until they open, then remove from their shells and use as above.

1 lb. wholewheat tagliatelle or fettuccine

½ stick (¼ cup) butter

1 onion, chopped

2–3 garlic cloves, crushed

¼ lb. bacon, diced

⅓ cup grated Bel Paese cheese

¾ cup grated sharp Cheddar cheese

¾ cup grated Gruyère cheese

1 cup grated Parmesan cheese

1¼ cups heavy cream

2 tablespoons chopped parsley

2 tablespoons chopped chives

1 tablespoon chopped basil

salt

Serves 4–6
Preparation time: 5 minutes
Cooking time: 8–12 minutes

1 Bring a large pot of salted water to a boil. Add the pasta and cook for 8–12 minutes or according to the package instructions, until just tender.

2 Meanwhile, melt half the butter in a pan, add the onion and garlic, and cook, without browning, for 2–3 minutes. Add the bacon and cook for 5 minutes, stirring occasionally. Stir in the cheeses and cream. Remove from the heat.

3 Drain the pasta thoroughly and turn into a warmed serving dish. Add the remaining butter and toss well. Return the sauce to the heat and stir in the herbs. Pour it over the pasta and mix well. Serve immediately.

tagliatelle with four cheeses

14 oz. penne

3 tablespoons oil

2 tablespoons butter

½ onion, chopped

1 small carrot, finely sliced

1 celery stalk, sliced

¼ lb. Italian sausage, skinned and crumbled

½ small yellow bell pepper, cored, seeded, and diced

4 basil leaves, torn

¼ cup dry red wine

2 tablespoons grated Romano cheese

2 tablespoons grated Parmesan cheese

basil leaves, for garnishing

1 Bring a large pot of salted water to a boil. Add the pasta and cook for 8–12 minutes or according to the package instructions, until just tender.

2 Meanwhile, heat the oil and the butter in a skillet, add the onion, carrot, and celery, and cook over low heat for 4 minutes.

3 Add the crumbled sausage, diced pepper, and torn basil, and mix well. Cook over medium heat for 3–4 minutes until the sausage has browned. Add the red wine.

4 Drain the pasta and transfer it to a warmed serving dish. Pour the sausage and vegetable sauce over it. Sprinkle with the cheeses and mix well before serving, garnished with whole basil leaves.

Serves 4
Preparation time: 10 minutes
Cooking time: 8–12 minutes

penne with spicy sausage sauce

smoked haddock & pepper pasta

1 Rinse the haddock, then pour boiling water over it and leave it for 2 minutes. Rinse again, then put into a pan, cover with the milk and bring to a boil. Reduce the heat and simmer for 10–15 minutes. Strain, reserving the milk, and let cool.

2 Heat the oil in another pan, add the shallots and garlic, and cook gently for 5 minutes until softened. Add the peppers and cook gently for 5–6 minutes, stirring occasionally.

3 Stir ½ cup of the strained milk into the cream, then mix in the cheese. Add more milk if it is too thick: it should be the consistency of sour cream. Purée the shallots and peppers with the cheese mixture in a food processor or blender, or simply stir the cream into the peppers. Return to the pan and add the tarragon and pepper. Taste the sauce, and add the sugar if necessary.

4 Bring a large pot of salted water to a boil. Add the pasta and cook for 8–12 minutes or according to the package instructions, until just tender.

5 Skin, bone, and flake the fish. Add it to the sauce and stir well. Drain the pasta and return it to the pan, along with half the butter. Whisk the rest of the butter into the simmering sauce. Pile the pasta into a warmed dish, pour the sauce over it, and serve at once.

1 lb. smoked haddock fillets or other smoked fish

2½ cups milk

2 tablespoons olive oil

3 shallots, finely chopped

2–3 garlic cloves, finely chopped

2 large red bell peppers, cored, seeded, and finely sliced

¼ cup sour cream

½ cup low-fat cream cheese

1 tablespoon chopped tarragon

¼–½ teaspoon sugar (optional)

8 oz. farfalle or conchiglie

2 tablespoons butter

salt and pepper

Serves 4–6
Preparation time: 15 minutes
Cooking time: 40 minutes

macaroni & cheese

1 Bring a large pot of salted water to a boil. Add the pasta and cook for 8–12 minutes or according to the package instructions, until just tender. Drain thoroughly. Return the pasta to the pot, add half the butter, and toss to mix.

2 Melt the remaining butter in a pan, add the flour, and stir over low heat for 2 minutes. Gradually stir in the milk and bring to a boil, stirring or whisking constantly. Cook for 2 minutes, then stir in the mustard, Tabasco, and Worcestershire sauce. Add the Cheddar, and stir until it has melted.

3 Fold in the macaroni. Spoon into a buttered ovenproof dish, and sprinkle with the breadcrumbs and Parmesan. Arrange the sliced tomato over the top, if using. Bake in a preheated oven at 400°F for 25–30 minutes, until hot and golden brown. Serve at once.

8 oz. macaroni

½ stick (¼ cup) butter

¼ cup flour

2 cups milk

1 generous teaspoon English mustard or other strong mustard

dash of Tabasco sauce

dash of Worcestershire sauce

¼ cup grated sharp Cheddar cheese

¼ cup dry breadcrumbs

½ cup grated Parmesan cheese

1 tomato, sliced (optional)

Serves 4

Preparation time: 10 minutes

Cooking time: 40–50 minutes

spinach cannelloni •

spaghetti with olive oil & garlic •

tortellini with ricotta & spinach •

tagliatelle with radicchio & cream •

spinach gnocchi gratin •

wholewheat pasta with broccoli & blue cheese •

eggplant layer bake •

fettuccine with chanterelles •

zucchini & red pesto pasta •

no-meat
meals

spinach cannelloni

1 Bring a large pot of salted water to a boil. Add half the lasagne sheets and cook for 8–12 minutes or according to the package instructions, until just tender. Remove with a slotted spoon and drain on paper towels. Repeat with the rest of the lasagne sheets.

2 Meanwhile, make the filling. Mix the ricotta, spinach, egg, flour, and garlic purée in a bowl. Add salt and pepper to taste. Spoon into a pastry bag fitted with a large plain nozzle. Set aside.

3 Make the sauce. Heat the oil in a pan and fry the onion until softened. Stir in the tomato sauce, and herbs, and simmer for 5 minutes.

4 Pipe the filling along the width of each pasta sheet, then roll them up to make filled cannelloni tubes. Arrange the tubes on the bottom of a lightly greased 2-quart, rectangular, ovenproof dish. Pour the sauce over the top, and cover with the grated mozzarella. Bake in a preheated oven at 375°F for 45 minutes.

12 sheets wide spinach lasagne

Filling:

12 oz. ricotta cheese (about 1½ cups)

4 oz. frozen chopped spinach, thawed (about ½ cup)

1 egg, beaten

¼ cup flour

2 tablespoons garlic purée

salt and pepper

Sauce and Topping:

1 tablespoon olive oil

1 onion, chopped

18 oz. tomato sauce (2¼ cups)

2 teaspoons mixed dried herbs

½ lb. mozzarella cheese, grated

Serves 4
Preparation time: 20 minutes
Cooking time: 1¼ hours

1 Bring a large pot of salted water to a boil. Add the pasta and cook for 8–12 minutes or according to the package instructions, until just tender. Drain thoroughly.

2 Heat the oil in the empty pasta pot and add the garlic and chiles, if using. Cook over medium heat, stirring constantly, until sizzling. Season the oil generously with salt and pepper.

3 Tip the pasta into the pot and toss to coat each strand in the flavored oil. Serve at once, sprinkled with more pepper.

12 oz. spaghetti

5 tablespoons extra virgin olive oil

4 garlic cloves, chopped

1–2 dried red chiles, finely chopped (optional)

salt and pepper

Serves 4

Preparation time: 5 minutes

Cooking time: 10–14 minutes

spaghetti with olive oil & garlic

It is worth using extra virgin olive oil for this recipe. This type of olive oil is produced from the first pressing of the olives, so it has a lovely green color and a full flavor.

tortellini with ricotta & spinach

1 Melt half the butter in a large frying pan, add the spinach, and toss thoroughly. Season well with salt and pepper. Sauté the spinach for 2 minutes, stirring constantly.

2 Bring a large pot of salted water to a boil. Add the pasta and cook for 5–10 minutes or according to package instructions, until just tender. Drain thoroughly and toss in the remaining butter.

3 Stir the ricotta and half of the Parmesan into the spinach mixture, then stir in the pasta. Transfer to a warmed serving dish, sprinkle with the remaining Parmesan, and serve at once.

1 stick (½ cup) butter

8 oz. frozen chopped spinach, thawed (about 1 cup)

1 lb. fresh tortellini

½ cup ricotta cheese

1 cup grated Parmesan cheese

salt and pepper

Serves 4
Preparation time: 5 minutes
Cooking time: 10–12 minutes

1 Melt the butter with the oil in a large, heavy frying pan. Add the onion and cook gently for 10 minutes, stirring occasionally, until it is soft.

2 Add the radicchio and cook, stirring, over medium heat until it wilts and starts to brown. Season with salt and pepper to taste. Add the cream and heat thoroughly.

3 Bring a large pot of salted water to a boil. Add the pasta and cook for 2–3 minutes, until just tender. Drain the pasta and place in a warmed serving dish. Pour the sauce over it, and add the Parmesan. Toss quickly to combine, and serve at once.

½ stick (¼ cup) butter

1 tablespoon olive oil

1 onion, finely chopped

8 oz. radicchio, finely shredded (about 4 cups)

⅔ cup cream

12 oz. fresh tagliatelle or fettuccine

1 cup grated Parmesan cheese

salt and pepper

Serves 4
Preparation time: 10 minutes
Cooking time: 15–17 minutes

tagliatelle with radicchio & cream

1 Wash the spinach and remove the stalks. Place the spinach in a large pot with just the water that clings to the leaves, and cook gently for 3–4 minutes until wilted. Drain in a colander, pressing out all the moisture. Finely chop the spinach, then put it in the bottom of a 2-quart ovenproof dish, and season with salt and pepper.

2 Bring a large pot of salted water to a boil, add the gnocchi in batches, and cook for just a few minutes. When they pop up to the surface, lift them out with a slotted spoon and drain on paper towels. Arrange the gnocchi over the spinach. Pour the tomato sauce over the gnocchi, and set aside while preparing the white sauce.

3 Melt the butter in a small saucepan. Add the flour and stir over low heat for 2 minutes. Stir in the milk and bring to a boil, stirring or whisking constantly. Cook for 2 minutes, then stir in the cheese, and season with salt and pepper. Pour the sauce over the gnocchi. Sprinkle with nutmeg and cook in a preheated oven at 400°F for 15 minutes, until golden. Serve garnished with radicchio leaves.

13 oz. fresh spinach (about 8 cups)

2 lbs. fresh spinach gnocchi

13 oz. jar tomato sauce with basil

1 tablespoon butter

2 tablespoons flour

1¼ cups milk

4 oz. blue Brie cheese, crumbled (about 1 cup)

freshly grated nutmeg

salt and pepper

radicchio leaves, for garnishing

Serves 4–6

Preparation time: 5 minutes

Cooking time: 30 minutes

spinach gnocchi gratin

wholewheat pasta with broccoli & blue cheese

8 oz. wholewheat conchiglie (shells)

about 4 cups small broccoli flowerets

¼ lb. blue cheese, crumbled (about 1 cup)

½ stick (¼ cup) butter

½ cup heavy cream or crème fraîche

salt and pepper

Serves 4
Preparation time: 5 minutes
Cooking time: 10–15 minutes

1 Bring a large pot of salted water to a boil. Add the pasta and cook for 8–12 minutes or according to the package instructions, until just tender. About 3 minutes before the end of the cooking time, add the broccoli to the pot and cook until both the pasta and the broccoli are tender. Drain well and keep warm.

2 Put the pot back on the heat and add the blue cheese, butter, and cream or crème fraîche. Heat gently, stirring all the time to make a smooth sauce. Taste, and adjust the seasoning if necessary.

3 Return the pasta and broccoli to the pot, toss thoroughly to mix with the sauce, then turn the mixture on to a warmed serving dish and serve immediately.

2 medium eggplants, sliced

2 tablespoons olive oil

1 onion, chopped

1 tablespoon chopped oregano

1 tablespoon chopped basil

¼ lb. white mushrooms, cut into quarters (about 1 cup)

18 oz. tomato sauce

9 fresh lasagne sheets

¾ lb. mozzarella cheese, sliced

¼ lb. grated Gruyère cheese (about 1 cup)

salt and pepper

Serves 4

Preparation time: 30 minutes

Cooking time: 1 hour 10 minutes

1 Spread out the eggplant slices on baking sheets. Sprinkle with 2 tablespoons salt and set aside for 15 minutes.

2 Heat 1 tablespoon of the oil in a large frying pan. Add the onion and cook for 3–5 minutes, stirring, until softened. Add the herbs, mushrooms, and tomato sauce. Simmer for 10 minutes, then add salt and pepper to taste.

3 Rinse the eggplant slices under plenty of cold running water, drain, and pat dry with paper towels. Spread them on the baking sheets and brush with the remaining oil. Broil under a high heat for 10 minutes, turning once. Remove from heat.

4 Arrange 3 lasagne sheets on the bottom of a lightly greased, rectangular, 2-quart ovenproof dish. Spoon onto them one-third of the tomato sauce. Place a layer of eggplant on top, and add one-third of the mozzarella and Gruyère. Repeat the layers twice more. Cover with foil. Bake in a preheated oven at 375°F for 45 minutes, removing the foil after 20 minutes to let the top brown and the cheese melt completely.

eggplant layer bake

fettuccine with chanterelles

1 Thinly slice the chanterelles, and set aside any discarded pieces of stem or peel. Pour the stock into a saucepan and bring to a boil. Add the mushroom peelings and cook over medium-high heat until reduced to ½ cup. Strain through a strainer or cheesecloth and discard the mushroom peelings.

2 Melt the butter with the oil in a large frying pan. Add the mushrooms and scallions and cook, stirring, until the mushrooms begin to render liquid. Add the wine and cook over high heat until the liquid has nearly evaporated.

3 Bring a large pot of salted water to a boil. Add the pasta and cook for 2–3 minutes, or until just tender. Meanwhile, add the reduced stock and cream to the mushroom mixture. Bring to a boil and reduce the sauce to half its original volume. Season to taste with salt and pepper.

4 Drain the pasta, add it to the frying pan along with the pine nuts, and toss to coat evenly with the sauce. Serve at once.

10 oz. chanterelles, morels, or other wild mushrooms

2 cups vegetable stock

1 tablespoon butter

1 tablespoon olive oil

1 bunch of scallions, finely chopped

¼ cup dry white wine

10 oz. fresh spinach fettuccine

1½ cups whipping cream or crème fraîche

2 tablespoons toasted pine nuts

salt and pepper

Serves 4
Preparation time: 15 minutes
Cooking time: 30 minutes

Wild mushrooms give this dish a wonderful flavor. However, cultivated mushrooms may be used, if wild mushrooms are not available.

1 Bring a large pot of salted water to a boil. Add the pasta and cook for 8–12 minutes or according to the package instructions, until just tender.

2 Meanwhile, heat 2 tablespoons of the oil in a deep frying pan, add the garlic, lemon zest, chile, and zucchini, and fry for 2–3 minutes until the zucchini is golden.

3 Drain the cooked pasta thoroughly and add to the zucchini pan, along with the remaining oil, the basil, red pesto, and plenty of pepper. Toss well over low heat to warm through gently for 1 minute, and serve at once.

12 oz. penne or other shapes

6 tablespoons olive oil

2 garlic cloves, sliced

1 teaspoon grated lemon zest

1 dried red chile, seeded and crushed

1 lb. zucchini, thinly sliced

1 tablespoon shredded basil leaves

2–3 tablespoons red pesto

salt and pepper

Serves 4
Preparation time: 10 minutes
Cooking time: 10–14 minutes

zucchini & red pesto pasta

chicken & pasta shell soup •

gnocchi & prosciutto bake •

cannelloni with peas, mushrooms, & ham •

lasagne marinara •

lamb chops with red wine sauce & pasta •

asian-flavored pappardelle •

baked pasta with pepper sauce •

rigatoni with anchovy sauce •

liver stroganoff •

spicy beef bake •

seafood pasta with ginger •

hearty dishes

1 tablespoon olive oil

1 garlic clove, crushed

2 onions, sliced into rings

1 teaspoon ground coriander

2 carrots, cut into thin sticks

¼ lb. cooked chicken breast, shredded

1 tablespoon tomato paste

5 cups hot chicken stock

3 oz. conchiglie or other small shells (about 1 cup)

3 oz. mozzarella cheese, cubed (about 1 cup)

2 tablespoons chopped parsley

1 teaspoon cayenne pepper

salt

crusty bread, for serving (optional)

1 Heat the oil in a large pot, add the garlic and onions, and cook for 2 minutes, stirring. Stir in the coriander, then add the carrots and chicken. Fry over medium heat for 3 minutes.

2 Stir in the tomato paste, stock, and a pinch of salt; bring to a boil. Add the pasta, lower the heat, and cook for 8–12 minutes or according to the package instructions, until just tender.

3 Add the mozzarella and parsley, stir well, then sprinkle with cayenne pepper. Serve in heated bowls, with crusty bread, if you like.

Serves 4
Preparation time: 15 minutes
Cooking time: 13–15 minutes

chicken & pasta shell soup

gnocchi & prosciutto bake

1 Heat the oil in a large pan, add the onion and garlic, and cook for 5 minutes, stirring, until softened. Add a pinch of tarragon.

2 Put the drained tomatoes and mascarpone in a food processor and blend to a smooth sauce. Stir the sauce into the onion mixture, add the sun-dried tomato paste, and season well. Simmer gently.

3 Bring a large pot of salted water to a boil, add the gnocchi in batches and cook for just a few minutes. When they pop up to the surface, lift them out with a slotted spoon and drain on paper towels.

4 Transfer the gnocchi to a large ovenproof dish and pour the tomato sauce over them. Stir the Cheddar and breadcrumbs together, and scatter the mixture over the top. Tear the prosciutto into thin lengths and lay it over the topping. Scatter the olives on top, season, and sprinkle on a little more tarragon. Bake in a preheated oven at 350°F for 20–25 minutes or until the top is bubbling and golden.

2 tablespoons olive oil

1 red onion, cut in half and sliced

2 garlic cloves, crushed

2 pinches of dried tarragon

15 oz. can tomatoes, drained

8 oz. mascarpone cheese

1 generous tablespoon sun-dried tomato paste

1 lb. fresh gnocchi

1 cup grated Cheddar cheese

1⅓ cups fresh white breadcrumbs

3 or 4 slices prosciutto

10 pitted green olives

salt and pepper

Serves 4

Preparation time: 5 minutes

Cooking time: 35–40 minutes

cannelloni with peas, mushrooms, & ham

1 Bring a large pot of salted water to a boil, add the lasagne sheets in batches, cook until just tender and drain well. Meanwhile, cook the frozen peas in a pot of boiling salted water according to package instructions and drain. Melt the butter for the filling in a frying pan, add the mushrooms, and fry gently until tender.

2 To make the white sauce, melt the butter in a small saucepan and stir in the flour. Cook gently, stirring, for 1–2 minutes. Remove from heat and slowly beat in the milk. Return to the heat and bring slowly to a boil, stirring all the time, until thick and smooth. Season to taste.

3 Place 2 tablespoons of the white sauce in a bowl, and beat in the egg and the egg yolk. Add two-thirds of the cheese, plus all of the ham, peas, and mushrooms. Season with salt, pepper, and nutmeg to taste, and mix well.

4 Spoon a little of the filling down one long side of each sheet of lasagne, and roll up each one into a cylinder. Arrange the cylinders in a buttered, ovenproof dish, coat with the remaining white sauce, and sprinkle with the remaining Parmesan. Bake in a preheated oven at 400°F, for about 20 minutes, until the top is golden. Serve hot, garnished with chopped parsley.

12 sheets wide lasagne

parsley, chopped, for garnishing

Filling:

1 cup small frozen peas

2 tablespoons butter

½ lb. mushrooms, thinly sliced (about 2⅔ cups)

1 egg, plus 1 egg yolk

1½ cups grated Parmesan cheese

½ lb. lean cooked ham, finely diced (about 2 cups)

grated nutmeg

salt and pepper

White Sauce:

2 tablespoons butter

¼ cup flour

2 cups milk

Serves 4
Preparation time: 15 minutes
Cooking time: 30 minutes

lasagne marinara

1 First make the sauce. Melt the butter in a saucepan, add the flour, and stir over low heat for 2 minutes. Gradually stir in the milk and bring to a boil, stirring or whisking constantly. Cook for 2 minutes. Pound the saffron strands to a powder using a mortar and pestle, and stir in 2–3 tablespoons boiling water until the saffron dissolves. Add to the sauce, and season to taste with salt and pepper.

2 Remove any bones from the salmon and cod, and cut the fish into bite-sized pieces. Add the fish and squid rings to the sauce and gently combine. Remove from the heat.

3 Spoon one-third of the fish mixture over the bottom of a 2-quart ovenproof dish, and then cover with a layer of lasagne sheets. Repeat these layers twice, finishing with a layer of lasagne sheets. Beat the eggs and Cheddar together in a bowl. Add salt and pepper to taste, and pour the mixture over the top of the lasagne.

4 Bake in a preheated oven at 375°F for 45 minutes; cover the dish with foil after 30 minutes if the surface starts to overbrown. Serve garnished with dill sprigs.

9 lasagne sheets, cooked acccording to package instructions

2 eggs, beaten

½ lb. Cheddar cheese, grated (about 2 cups)

dill sprigs, for garnishing

Sauce:

½ stick (¼ cup) butter

½ cup flour

2½ cups milk

a few saffron strands

½ lb. fresh salmon

¼ lb. cod fillet

¼ lb. fresh squid rings

salt and pepper

Serves 4
Preparation time: 10 minutes
Cooking time: 55 minutes

1 Trim any excess fat from the chops. Fry them with the garlic in a non-stick frying pan over medium heat, for 3 minutes on each side. Transfer the chops to a casserole dish. Discard any fat remaining in the pan.

2 Melt the butter in the pan, add the zucchini and mushrooms, and cook, stirring them once or twice, for 2 minutes. Add them to the chops. Add the tomatoes, honey, wine, marjoram, and salt and pepper to taste. Cover the casserole dish and cook in a preheated oven at 375°F for 25 minutes.

3 About 15 minutes before the chops are ready, bring a large pot of salted water to a boil. Add the pasta and cook for 8–12 minutes or according to the package instructions, until just tender. Drain thoroughly.

4 Remove the casserole from the oven and garnish with chopped parsley. Serve with the pasta.

4 large loin lamb chops or 8 small ones

1 garlic clove, finely chopped

2 tablespoons butter

2 small zucchini, sliced

6 oz. white mushrooms, sliced (about 1¾ cups)

4 large tomatoes, skinned and sliced

1 tablespoon honey

⅔ cup red wine

1 tablespoon chopped marjoram

12 oz. wholewheat pasta

salt and pepper

1 tablespoon chopped parsley, for garnishing

Serves 4

Preparation time: 15 minutes

Cooking time: 35 minutes

lamb chops with red wine sauce & pasta

asian-flavored pappardelle

1 Bring a large pot of salted water to a boil. Add the pasta and cook for 8–12 minutes or according to the package instructions, until just tender.

2 Meanwhile, heat a wok. Add the oil and heat over medium heat until hot. Add the meat and fry for 1 minute. Add the ginger and almost all of the scallions, and stir-fry for 2 minutes. Add the chile, hoisin sauce, soy sauce, lime juice and zest, and the coconut milk, and cook for 1 minute.

3 Drain the pasta and turn into a large bowl. Fold in half of the meat and spoon into a large ovenproof dish. Spoon the remaining meat mixture over the dish and scatter with the rest of the scallions. Cook in a preheated oven at 350°F for 10 minutes, until the meat starts to become crisp.

4 Remove the dish from the oven and scatter the coriander leaves over the top. Serve with lime wedges.

8 oz. pappardelle (or other broad egg noodles)

2 tablespoons oil

¾ lb. cooked duck, turkey, or chicken

2 inch piece of fresh ginger, peeled and finely chopped

1 bunch of scallions, cut into long lengths

1 fresh red chile, seeded and chopped

3 tablespoons hoisin sauce

good splash of dark soy sauce

juice and zest of 1 lime

1¼ cups coconut milk

salt

coriander leaves, for garnishing

lime wedges, for serving

Serves 6

Preparation time: 10 minutes

Cooking time: 20–25 minutes

1 Place the peppers in a pot with the onion, tomatoes and a pinch of salt; cover, and simmer for about 5 minutes. Add the stock, bring to a boil, and simmer for a further 15 minutes.

2 Meanwhile, bring a large pot of salted water to a boil. Add the pasta and cook for 8–12 minutes or according to the package instructions, until just tender. Drain thoroughly.

3 Sprinkle the basil over the pepper sauce, adjust the seasoning to taste, then mix with the drained pasta and the diced mozzarella. Transfer to a large greased ovenproof dish, pour the milk over it, and cook in a preheated oven at 400°F for 15 minutes, or until golden brown. Serve garnished with shredded basil leaves.

2 large yellow bell peppers, cored, seeded, and finely chopped

½ onion, thinly sliced

6 plum tomatoes, skinned and chopped

1 cup vegetable stock

12 oz. penne or other pasta shapes

½ teaspoon chopped basil

½ lb. mozzarella cheese, diced (about 2 cups)

3 tablespoons milk

salt and pepper

shredded basil leaves, to garnish

Serves 4
Preparation time: 20 minutes
Cooking time: 35–40 minutes

baked pasta with pepper sauce

1 Broil the pepper under a preheated hot broiler, turning occasionally, until it is blistered and charred on all sides. Place in a plastic bag and leave until cool enough to handle. Strip off the skin and chop the flesh.

2 Heat the oil in a pot, add the chopped pepper and garlic, and cook for 3 minutes, stirring. Add the tomatoes, anchovies, wine, and sugar, and season with pepper. Simmer for 15–20 minutes until thickened.

3 Meanwhile, bring a large pot of salted water to a boil. Add the pasta and cook for 8–12 minutes or according to the package instructions, until just tender. Drain thoroughly.

4 To serve, divide the rigatoni among 4 warmed serving dishes, and top with the sauce. Garnish with Parmesan and chopped parsley.

1 red bell pepper

¼ cup olive oil

2 garlic cloves, finely chopped

6 tomatoes, skinned and chopped

2 oz. canned anchovy fillets, rinsed and finely chopped (about ⅓ cup)

¼ cup dry white wine

1 teaspoon light brown sugar

12 oz. rigatoni

salt and pepper

To Garnish:

grated Parmesan cheese

chopped fresh parsley

Serves 4	
Preparation time: 25 minutes	
Cooking time: 25–30 minutes	

rigatoni with anchovy sauce

liver stroganoff

1 Melt the butter in a large frying pan, add the onion, and cook over low heat until soft. Add the liver and cook for 5 minutes, stirring constantly.

2 Stir in the mushrooms, tomato paste, Worcestershire sauce, lemon juice, and salt and pepper to taste; then cook for a further 5 minutes, stirring occasionally.

3 Bring a large pot of salted water to a boil. Add the pasta and cook for 8–12 minutes or according to the package instructions, until just tender. Drain thoroughly.

4 Remove the liver pan from the heat. Stir the cream into the pan, return the pan to a low heat, and warm through without boiling. Taste, and adjust the seasoning, then serve with the pasta.

2 tablespoons butter

1 onion, chopped

1 lb. lamb's or calf's liver, sliced into very thin strips

½ lb. white mushrooms, sliced (about 2⅓ cups)

1 tablespoon tomato paste

1 tablespoon Worcestershire sauce

¼ cup lemon juice

8 oz. pasta twists

⅔ cup sour cream

salt and pepper

Serves 4

Preparation time: 15 minutes

Cooking time: 15–20 minutes

spicy beef bake

1 Bring a large pot of salted water to a boil. Add the pasta and cook for 8–12 minutes or according to the package instructions, until just tender.

2 Meanwhile, heat the oil in a frying pan, add the shallots, cumin, and chile, and cook for 2 minutes, stirring. Add the beef and cook over high heat for 5 minutes, turning constantly. Stir in the chopped cilantro. Add the chickpeas, lentils, tomato paste, and mesquite sauce. Simmer for 2 minutes.

3 Drain the pasta and return it to the pot. Toss in a little oil. Stir the meat mixture into the pasta, then transfer it to a buttered, 2-quart, ovenproof dish. Sprinkle with the grated Emmental, and cook in a preheated oven at 350°F for 25 minutes.

8 oz. three-color farfalle (bows)

2 tablespoons oil, plus extra for tossing the pasta

2 shallots (or 1 small mild onion), finely chopped

pinch of ground cumin

1 dried chile

½ lb. lean ground beef

2–3 oz. fresh cilantro, chopped (about a half a bunch)

15 oz. can chickpeas, drained

15 oz. can lentils, drained

2 tablespoons tomato paste

8 oz. jar mesquite sauce

¾ cup grated Emmental cheese

Serves 6
Preparation time: 10 minutes
Cooking time: 40 minutes

■ Mesquite sauce is a hot, spicy sauce with a smoky flavor which hails from Mexico and Texas. It is named after the mesquite tree, whose wood is used for smoking and barbecuing foods.

seafood pasta with ginger

1 Place the mussels in a large pot. Scatter the ginger slices, shallots, and half of the garlic over the top, and sprinkle with the wine. Cover, and steam over medium-high heat for about 5 minutes until the mussels open. Discard the ginger slices. Remove the mussels with a slotted spoon. Pour the cooking juices into a small pan. Cook over high heat until the liquid is reduced to ½ cup. Cover and set aside. Remove the mussels from their shells and set aside.

2 Bring a large pot of salted water to a boil. Add the pasta and cook for 8–12 minutes or according to the package instructions, until just tender. Drain the pasta and transfer to a warmed serving dish.

3 Heat a wok over medium heat. When it is hot, add the oil and butter, then add the remaining garlic and the shredded ginger, and cook for 30 seconds until softened. Add the shrimp and cook for about 1 minute until they just begin to turn pink. Add the scallops, and toss to mix.

4 Pour in the reserved cooking juices and the cream or crème fraîche, then cook for about 1 minute until the sauce is reduced to a creamy consistency. Add the reserved mussels and lemon juice, and season with salt and pepper. Spoon the sauce over the pasta and serve at once, garnished with the deep-fried basil.

2 lb. fresh mussels, cleaned

4 slices of fresh ginger, peeled, plus 2 tablespoons finely shredded ginger

2 shallots (or 1 small mild onion), finely chopped

2 garlic cloves, finely chopped

½ cup dry white wine

12 oz. tagliarini or other thin, flat, ribbon noodles

1 tablespoon olive oil

2 tablespoons butter

½ lb. raw shrimp, peeled and deveined (about 2 cups)

½ lb. small scallops

½ cup heavy cream or crème fraîche

1–2 teaspoons lemon juice

salt and pepper

deep-fried basil leaves, for garnishing

Serves 4–6

Preparation time: 20 minutes

Cooking time: 25 minutes

baked stuffed mushrooms •

ginger & carrot pasta ribbons •

deep-fried pasta •

shrimp & apricot pasta salad •

green salad with walnuts & parmesan •

warm scallop & arugula salad •

chicken & mushroom penne salad •

pasta salad niçoise •

tuscan panzanella •

goat cheese & watercress conchiglie •

crunchy pasta salad •

seafood sauce •

italian vegetable sauce •

sauce alla amatriciana •

cilantro & walnut sauce •

fresh tomato sauce •

salads, sauces & side dishes

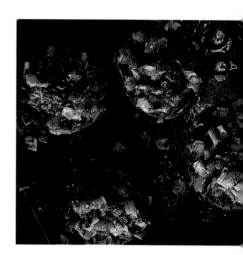

1 Bring a large pot of salted water to a boil. Add the pasta and cook for 8–12 minutes or according to the package instructions, until just tender. Drain thoroughly.

2 Chop the mushroom stems finely and set aside. Peel the mushrooms if blemished, and broil under medium heat for 5 minutes, until just softened. Remove and set aside.

3 Put the chopped onion into a large bowl. Add the chopped mushroom stems, cooked macaroni, walnuts, parsley, Cheddar cubes, and tomato paste. Mix well, then add enough of the beaten egg to bind the mixture. Season to taste with salt and pepper.

4 Divide the filling among the mushrooms, mounding the mixture up with a spoon. Drizzle a little olive oil over them. Arrange the filled mushrooms, far apart, on a broiler pan. Broil for 15–20 minutes, until the top of the stuffing is crisp and has started to char at the edges. Serve at once, garnished with lemon wedges.

2 oz. macaroni (about ⅔ cup)

4 large mushrooms, about 4–6 inches in diameter

1 small onion, very finely chopped

¼ cup chopped walnuts

1 tablespoon chopped parsley

¼ cup cubed Cheddar cheese

1 tablespoon tomato paste

1 egg, beaten

1 tablespoon olive oil

salt and pepper

lemon wedges, for garnishing

Serves 4

Preparation time: 10 minutes

Cooking time: 25–30 minutes

baked stuffed mushrooms

ginger & carrot pasta ribbons

1 Bring a large pot of salted water to a boil. Add the pasta and cook for 8–12 minutes or according to the package instructions, until just tender.

2 Meanwhile, using a potato peeler, shave the carrots into thin ribbons. Either melt the butter in a frying pan and sauté the carrots and ginger for 5 minutes, or steam them without the butter until tender.

3 Drain the pasta and return it to the rinsed-out pot. Toss with the oil and season with pepper. Carefully fold the carrot mixture into the cooked pasta. Sprinkle with pine nuts, and serve at once.

10 oz. pappardelle or other broad egg noodles

2 carrots

2 tablespoons butter (optional)

1-inch piece fresh ginger, peeled and grated

2 tablespoons olive oil

¼ cup pine nuts

salt and pepper

Serves 4

Preparation time: 10 minutes

Cooking time: 8–12 minutes

1 Dissolve the yeast and sugar in a little lukewarm water. Set aside for 10 minutes.

2 Sift the flour and a little salt into a bowl. Stir in the yeast mixture, then add the butter and enough stock to make a soft dough. Knead well, then roll it out to a fairly thick sheet on a lightly floured work surface.

3 Fold the 4 corners of the dough in towards the center, then flatten with the rolling pin. Fold and flatten again at least 5 more times. Roll out to a sheet about ¼ inch thick, and cut into small rectangles.

4 Heat the oil and deep fry the shapes a few at a time until golden brown and puffed up. Drain on paper towels while frying the remainder. Sprinkle with salt and pepper, and serve hot.

½ teaspoon dried yeast

¼ teaspoon sugar

4 cups flour

2 tablespoons butter

⅔ cup lukewarm chicken stock

vegetable oil, for deep frying

salt and pepper

Serves 6
Preparation time: 30 minutes, plus resting
Cooking time: 20–30 minutes

deep-fried pasta

■ These crisp, tasty puffs make excellent snacks with drinks, and are ideal for serving with savory sauces and dips.

shrimp & apricot pasta salad

1 Bring a large pot of salted water to a boil. Add the pasta and cook for 8–12 minutes or according to the package instructions, until just tender. Drain, refresh with cold water, and drain again.

2 To make the dressing, mix the yogurt, mayonnaise, grated cucumber, and mint. Season with salt and pepper to taste.

3 Mix the cold pasta with the shrimp, apricot, and cucumber slices. Fold in the dressing, chill lightly, then serve garnished with mint sprigs.

8 oz. conchiglie, or other shell pasta

¼ lb. cooked peeled shrimp (¾ cup)

4 fresh apricots, peeled, stoned and sliced

½ cucumber, cut in half and thinly sliced

mint sprigs, for garnishing

Dressing:

3 tablespoons plain yogurt

3 tablespoons mayonnaise

3 tablespoons grated cucumber

1 tablespoon chopped mint

salt and pepper

Serves 4
Preparation time: 15 minutes
Cooking time: 8–12 minutes

green salad with walnuts & parmesan

1 If the salad leaves are large, tear them roughly, and place them in a serving bowl with the onion.

2 In a dry pan, lightly toast the walnut pieces, then roughly chop them and let them cool.

3 To make the dressing, either whisk together all the ingredients in a small bowl, or place them in a screw-top jar and shake until blended.

4 Add the walnuts to the salad and pour the dressing over it. Toss lightly to mix. Use a small sharp knife to slice the Parmesan into very thin shavings. Sprinkle these over the salad, and serve at once.

large bowl of mixed salad leaves, (for example, arugula, lamb's lettuce, spring cabbage, red oak leaf, chicory, Belgian endive)

½ mild onion, chopped

½ cup walnut pieces

1½ oz. piece Parmesan cheese

Dressing:

5 tablespoons walnut oil

2 tablespoons red wine vinegar

½–1 teaspoon wholegrain mustard

pinch of sugar

salt and pepper

Serves 4–6

Preparation time: 10 minutes

Cooking time: 2–3 minutes

1   In a small bowl, combine the lemon juice and 2 tablespoons of the oil. Season to taste with salt and pepper. Set aside.

2   Heat the remaining oil in a frying pan over medium heat. Add the red peppers with a pinch of salt, and cook for about 5 minutes, stirring, until just tender. Transfer the peppers to a plate and set aside. Arrange the salad leaves on individual plates.

3   Rinse the scallops and pat dry with paper towels. Season them with salt and pepper and arrange in one layer in the top of a steamer, set over boiling water. Cover and steam over high heat for about 3 minutes, until tender. Drain on paper towels.

4   To serve, arrange the warm scallops on the salad leaves. Arrange the red peppers, olives, capers, and chives around the scallops. Whisk the dressing, and spoon it over the salad. Serve at once.

2 tablespoons lemon juice

3 tablespoons olive oil

2 red bell peppers, cored, seeded, and cut into thin strips

mixed salad leaves

¾ lb. scallops

⅓ cup pitted and quartered black olives

1 tablespoon capers

2 tablespoons chopped chives

salt and pepper

Serves 4	
Preparation time: 10–15 minutes	
Cooking time: 8 minutes	

warm scallop & arugula salad

■ This salad would make a good starter before a light pasta main-course dish. Alternatively, serve with spaghetti dressed with a simple sauce.

chicken & mushroom penne salad

1 Bring a large pot of salted water to a boil. Add the pasta and cook for 8–12 minutes or according to the package instructions, until just tender.

2 Drain the pasta, rinse under cold running water in a colander, and drain again. Transfer the cooled pasta to a large salad bowl.

3 Add the chicken, mushrooms, and red pepper, along with the oil, sesame seeds, lemon juice, and scallions. Add salt and pepper to taste, and toss well. Garnish with the chopped parsley.

10 oz. penne

½ lb. cooked chicken breast, sliced into strips

¼ lb. mushrooms, sliced (1 cup)

1 red bell pepper, cored, seeded, and finely sliced

2 tablespoons sesame oil

1 teaspoon sesame seeds

1 tablespoon lemon juice

4 scallions, diagonally sliced

salt and pepper

2 tablespoons chopped parsley, for garnishing

Serves 4
Preparation time: 15 minutes
Cooking time: 8–12 minutes

pasta salad niçoise

1 Soak the anchovies in milk for 20 minutes to remove excess salt. Bring a large pot of salted water to a boil. Add the pasta and cook for 8–12 minutes or according to package instructions, until just tender. Drain, refresh in cold water, then drain again.

2 Meanwhile, cook the beans in salted boiling water for 3–4 minutes, until tender. Drain, refresh in cold water, then drain again.

3 Whisk the dressing ingredients together in a bowl. Stir in the pasta and beans, and mix well. Season with salt and pepper, then let cool.

4 Add the tomatoes, tuna, and herbs, and fold in gently. Transfer to a serving platter. Drain and dry the anchovies, and cut the fillets in half lengthwise. Arrange the anchovies, eggs, and olives over the top of the salad, and serve at once.

2 oz. can anchovies in oil, drained (about ⅓ cup)

a little milk

8 oz. farfalle (bows)

½ lb. green beans, topped and tailed

2 firm ripe tomatoes, skinned and cut into wedges

6 oz. can tuna, drained and flaked

2 tablespoons chopped mixed herbs (for example, tarragon, basil, parsley)

2 hard-boiled eggs, shelled and quartered

1 cup pitted black olives

salt and pepper

Dressing:

6 tablespoons olive oil

3 tablespoons tarragon vinegar

½ teaspoon mustard powder

pinch of sugar

Serves 4–6
Preparation time: 20 minutes
Cooking time: 8–12 minutes

tuscan panzanella

1 Scatter the bread cubes on a tray and leave them, uncovered, to harden overnight.

2 Put the tomatoes, cucumber, red pepper, onion, capers, and parsley into a large non-metallic bowl, and mix gently. In a small bowl, combine the vinegar, mustard, anchovies, if using, and oregano. Whisk in the oil. Season to taste with salt and pepper. Pour it over the mixed vegetables, and stir to mix. Cover, and let stand at room temperature for at least 1 hour.

3 About 20 minutes before serving, mix the bread cubes with the vegetables. Taste, and adjust the seasoning. To serve, transfer the salad to individual plates, and garnish with parsley sprigs.

8 oz. Italian country bread, crusts removed, cut into 1-inch cubes

3 large ripe tomatoes, skinned, seeded, and chopped

2 small cucumbers, peeled, seeded, and diced

1 red bell pepper, cored, seeded, and diced

1 small red onion, thinly sliced

3 tablespoons capers

1 oz. chopped parsley (about ½ cup)

¼ cup red wine vinegar

¼ cup Dijon mustard

2½ tablespoons finely chopped anchovies (optional)

2 teaspoons finely chopped oregano

1 cup olive oil

salt and pepper

parsley sprigs, for garnishing

Serves 4–6

Preparation time: 15 minutes, plus standing

goat cheese & watercress conchiglie

1 Bring a large pot of salted water to a boil. Add the pasta and cook for 8–12 minutes or according to the package instructions, until just tender. Drain the pasta, rinse under cold running water in a colander, and drain again. Transfer to a large salad bowl.

2 Mix the scallions, raspberry vinegar, and oil in a bowl. Add salt and pepper to taste. Pour the dressing over the pasta.

3 Fold in the goat cheese, the orange or grapefruit slices, and the watercress. Toss the salad and chill until needed.

10 oz. conchiglie

3 scallions, diagonally sliced

3 tablespoons raspberry vinegar

6 tablespoons olive oil

¼ lb. soft goat cheese, diced (about 1 cup)

1 orange or grapefruit, peeled and sliced into rings

1 bunch of watercress, washed and trimmed (if not available, use fresh spinach)

salt and pepper

Serves 4	
Preparation time: 10 minutes	
Cooking time: 8–12 minutes	

crunchy pasta salad

1 Bring a large pot of salted water to a boil. Add the pasta and cook for 8–12 minutes or according to the package instructions, until just tender.

2 Drain the pasta and rinse under cold running water in a colander. Drain again thoroughly, and transfer to a large salad bowl. Add the cabbage and celery.

3 Quarter the apple, slice it into a bowl, and sprinkle with lemon juice to prevent it from discoloring. Fold the apple slices into the pasta with the raisins. Mix together the mayonnaise and milk, add salt and pepper to taste, then fold it into the salad. Garnish with the cayenne pepper and celery leaves.

10 oz. conchiglie

¼ red cabbage, shredded

2 celery stalks, chopped

1 Granny Smith apple, cored

1 tablespoon lemon juice

2 tablespoons golden raisins

¼ cup mayonnaise

¼ cup milk

salt and pepper

For Garnishing:

pinch of cayenne pepper

celery leaves

Serves 4
Preparation time: 20 minutes
Cooking time: 8–12 minutes

seafood sauce

1 Melt the butter in a large saucepan, add the onion and garlic, and cook gently for 2 minutes, stirring. Add the flour, and stir over a low heat for 2 minutes. Gradually add the stock and the wine, and bring to a boil, stirring or whisking constantly.

2 Reduce the heat and stir in the halibut and scallops, and cook gently for 2–3 minutes.

3 Stir in the mussels, shrimp, and marjoram. Season to taste with salt and pepper, and heat gently for 1 minute. Just before serving over freshly cooked pasta, add the cream and heat through.

½ stick (¼ cup) butter

1 onion, finely chopped

1 garlic clove, crushed

½ cup flour

2 cups vegetable or fish stock

⅔ cup white wine

¼ lb. halibut, cubed

6 scallops, cut into quarters

2 oz. canned or frozen mussels

¼ lb. cooked peeled shrimp

1 tablespoon chopped marjoram

⅔ cup light cream

salt and pepper

Serves 4

Preparation time: 15 minutes

Cooking time: 10 minutes

1 tablespoon oil

1 onion, finely chopped

1 red bell pepper, cored, seeded, and finely chopped

1 yellow bell pepper, cored, seeded, and finely chopped

2 celery stalks, finely chopped

1 zucchini, finely chopped

4 tomatoes, skinned, seeded, and chopped

½ lb. spinach leaves, chopped

⅔ cup vegetable stock or water

1 teaspoon sugar

salt and pepper

1 Heat the oil in a large saucepan, add the onion, peppers, celery, and zucchini, and cook for 2 minutes, stirring, until almost tender.

2 Stir in the tomatoes, spinach, stock or water, and the sugar. Season to taste with salt and pepper.

3 Bring to a boil and cook for 10 minutes, until the sauce has reduced and thickened.

Serves 4
Preparation time: 15 minutes
Cooking time: 15 minutes

italian vegetable sauce

■ This is a great sauce to make when summer vegetables are plentiful. Serve as a topping to plain pasta, as illustrated, or use for layering in lasagne and other baked pasta dishes.

sauce alla amatriciana

1 Heat the oil in a heavy saucepan, add the bacon, and fry gently for 5 minutes until golden. Remove with a slotted spoon and keep warm.

2 In the same pan, fry the onion until transparent, then add the pimiento, tomatoes, and bacon. Season to taste with salt and pepper, then cook briskly for 10 minutes, stirring all the time. Serve hot over freshly cooked pasta, garnished with grated Parmesan or Romano cheese and cilantro sprigs.

1 tablespoon sunflower or olive oil

3 oz. lean bacon, diced (about 6–8 strips)

1 small onion, finely chopped

1 canned or bottled pimiento, chopped

¾ lb. fresh tomatoes, skinned and chopped (3 cups)

salt and pepper

For Garnishing:

grated Parmesan or Romano cheese

cilantro sprigs

Serves 4

Preparation time: 10 minutes

Cooking time: 20 minutes

cilantro & walnut sauce

1 Place the olive oil and cream in a bowl.

2 Add the cheese, walnuts, and chopped cilantro. Season with salt and pepper, and mix all the ingredients together thoroughly.

3 Pour the sauce over freshly cooked pasta, and stir well to combine. Garnish with cilantro sprigs and serve immediately.

1 tablespoon olive oil

¼ cup heavy cream

1¼ cups grated Cheddar cheese

¼ cup finely chopped walnuts

1 oz. cilantro, finely chopped (about ½ cup), plus extra sprigs for garnishing

salt and pepper

Serves 4
Preparation time: 5 minutes

■ This sauce can be made in advance and stored in the refrigerator in a covered container for 1-2 days.

1 tablespoon olive oil

1 celery stalk, chopped

1 carrot, chopped

2 onions, chopped

2 garlic cloves, crushed

2 lbs. large ripe tomatoes, quartered

2 teaspoons sugar

2 tablespoons chopped basil

salt and pepper

1 Heat the oil in a pot, add the celery, carrot, onions, and garlic, and cook gently for 3 minutes, stirring, until tender.

2 Stir in the tomatoes, sugar, basil, and salt and pepper to taste. Bring to a boil. Reduce the heat, cover the pot with a lid, and cook gently for 30 minutes.

3 Transfer the sauce to a food processor or blender, and blend until smooth. Reheat, and serve over freshly cooked pasta.

Serves 4–6
Preparation time: 10 minutes
Cooking time: 35 minutes

fresh tomato sauce

96

index